ANGELS
FOR KIDS

Dear Ava,

~~Happy~~ 1ST Communion's

always remember
that your guardian
angel is *always*
with you — guiding
and protecting you.
God Bless!
Miss Katie

ANGELS
FOR KIDS

DONNA-MARIE COOPER O'BOYLE

PARACLETE PRESS
BREWSTER, MASSACHUSETTS

2013 First printing

Angels for Kids

Copyright © 2013 by Donna-Marie Cooper O'Boyle

ISBN 978-1-61261-408-3

Scriptural references are taken from The Catholic Edition of the Revised Standard Version of the Bible, copyright © 1965, 1966 National Council of the Churches of Christ in the United States of America. Used by permission. All rights reserved.

The Paraclete Press name and logo (dove on cross) are trademarks of Paraclete Press, Inc.

Library of Congress Cataloging-in-Publication Data

O'Boyle, Donna-Marie Cooper.
 Angels for kids / Donna-Marie Cooper O'Boyle.
    pages cm
 Includes bibliographical references.
 ISBN 978-1-61261-408-3 (trade pb)
 1. Angels--Catholic Church. I. Title.
 BT966.3.O26 2013
 235'.3--dc23   2013025585

10 9 8 7 6 5 4 3 2 1

Published by Paraclete Press
Brewster, Massachusetts
www.paracletepress.com

Printed in the United States of America

Lovingly to my children

Justin, Chaldea, Jessica, Joseph, and Mary-Catherine

CONTENTS

WELCOME!

*A*ngels are real. We just can't see them. But that doesn't mean they aren't all around us.

I have been praying to my Guardian Angel ever since I was a little girl. I was a very lucky kid because my mother taught me to pray this prayer every morning and night:

> O angel of God, my guardian dear,
> To whom his love commits me here,
> Ever this day, be at my side,
> To watch and guard, to rule and guide.
> Amen.

I have always firmly believed that my Guardian Angel heard my prayers and helped me out each day. Sometimes he got me out of some pretty tricky situations, and I believe he still does. But not every kid knows about his or her Guardian Angel or about the zillions of other kinds of Angels working hard in heaven and on earth to carry out God's plans. That's sad.

I would love it if every kid in the whole world would join me in discovering the Angels, learning more about their fascinating lives, exploring their reality for themselves. I believe that by reading this book, your eyes and heart will be opened to the awesome splendor of holy Angels as you become more and more acquainted with them.

We are so privileged God has blessed us with the gift of Angels. Imagine how beautiful our world would be if everyone prayed to their Guardian Angels and listened to their holy guidance!

I hope you will enjoy this book. It is meant to be fun to read. But most of all, I hope that, by reading it, you will come even closer to the holy Angels that are all around us.

CHAPTER ONE

A MULTITUDE OF ANGELS

"Are not all angels spirits in the divine service,
sent to serve for the sake of those
who are to inherit salvation?"

HEBREWS 1:14

The invisible world of Angels is often over-
looked, though amazingly it has been with
us since the dawn of creation. Countless
Angels offer service and protection to humankind.
We just can't see it happening.

But before I tell you more about what the Angels are
and what they do, I'll tell you what they are not.

Angels are not fairies.

They are not make-believe. They are not a fantasy, a cartoon character, or a figment of someone's imagination. Angels are not fictitious—at all. Angels are real! They are intelligent heavenly spirits who constantly behold the face of God. That's certainly incredible to ponder!

God created the Angels before he created the physical universe and before he created humankind. The Angels shouted for joy when God created the earth (Job 38: 4, 7). Our Church teaches us, "We firmly believe and profess, without qualification, that there is only one true God . . . Creator of all things visible and invisible, spiritual and corporeal, who by His almighty power, from the very beginning of time, has created both orders of creatures in the same way out of nothing." God made the Angels and people out of nothing! Just think about that for a moment.

Some people refuse to believe that there are Angels, and some people have not yet been convinced that they exist. Blessed Pope John Paul II pointed out in his study called "Catechesis on the Angels" that the existence of Angels was denied even in Christ's time by people called the Sadducees. The Holy Pontiff went on to explain that the reality of Angels has been continually denied in every age since that time.

We only need to look to the Scriptures for proof of the reality of Angels. Sacred Scripture identifies nine choirs (or types) of Angels. And Jesus spoke of more than twelve legions of Angels. When Jesus was arrested after praying in the Garden of Gethsemane, he said, "Do you think that I cannot appeal to my Father, and he will at once send me more than twelve legions of angels?" (Matthew 26:53).

Jesus also spoke about the Angels of the innocent and the Angels who will separate the good from the bad on the last day. Jesus's disciples asked Jesus to explain the parable of the weeds of the field. Jesus told them that he sows the good seeds and the devil sows bad seeds. Jesus said that when he comes back to earth at the end of the world, he will "send his angels, and they will collect out of the kingdom all causes of sin and all evildoers, and they will throw them into the furnace of fire, where there will be weeping and gnashing of teeth. Then the righteous will shine like the sun in the kingdom of their Father" (Matthew 13:41–43). These words are powerful and give us much to think about as to how we are living our lives.

Angels are mentioned in both the Old Testament and the New Testament of the Bible, where we learn that Angels worked throughout history as intermediaries between God and people. We'll look at that in greater depth in chapter two.

Saint Thomas Aquinas said, "The Angels work together for the benefit of us all." We are very blessed indeed because God decided to create the Angels. The good Angels now live in heaven, adoring God constantly. They also have many other tasks and responsibilities, which we'll talk about throughout this book.

Angels are not all the same.

There are many different kinds of Angels. We could never count them all.

Theologians like Saint Thomas Aquinas looked at what the Bible says about Angels and began to imagine three groups, or hierarchies, of Angels. Within each hierarchy are three categories. The first hierarchy is called the "Heavenly Counselors of God." These Angels are always in God's presence. They don't have contact with people on earth. The three categories in this group are "Seraphim," "Cherubim," and "Thrones."

The second hierarchy is called "Heavenly Governors." Their job is to regulate the forces of nature all around us in the universe, including on earth. Their three categories are "Dominions," "Virtues," and "Powers."

HIERARCHY

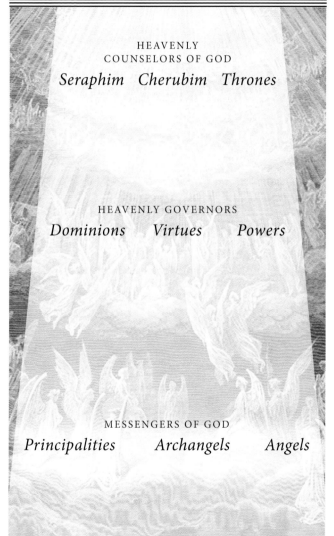

**HEAVENLY
COUNSELORS OF GOD**

Seraphim   Cherubim   Thrones

HEAVENLY GOVERNORS

Dominions   Virtues   Powers

MESSENGERS OF GOD

Principalities   Archangels   Angels

The third hierarchy of Angels is known as "Messengers of God." This hierarchy of Angels deals directly with people on earth. The three categories of this hierarchy are "Principalities," "Archangels," and "Angels." Each of these categories is called a "choir." So, we can say that there are nine choirs of Angels, all mentioned in the Bible, and all playing their essential roles in the universe, before God, and with us!

Angels are not silent.

The Catechism of the Catholic Church tells us, "The Church venerates the angels who help her on her earthly pilgrimage and protect every human being" (§352). Saint Basil the Great taught us that the Angels are part of God's plan of salvation. Saint Basil proclaimed, "Beside each believer stands an angel as a protector and shepherd leading him to life." This is how we each are so very privileged to have a Guardian Angel whom we can call our own.

Saint Ambrose encouraged us to pray to and communicate with the Angels. Later in this book, you'll see some special prayers that you can offer to them. You can also simply speak to the Angels in your own words and ask them to protect and guide you. This is true especially of your Guardian Angel, who is always near you and ready to assist you.

CHAPTER TWO

ANGELS IN THE BIBLE

"Then the devil left him, and suddenly angels came and waited on him"

MATTHEW 4:11

We can find Angels in the Bible from the beginning to the very end (from Genesis to Revelation). In the beginning of the Bible, in the story of Adam and Eve, we read, "Therefore the LORD God sent him forth from the Garden of Eden, to till the ground from which he was taken. He drove out the man; and at the east of the garden of Eden he placed the cherubim, and a sword flaming and turning to guard the way to the tree of life" (Genesis 3:23–24).

Then, at the end, in the book of Revelation, we read:

And all the angels stood around the throne and around the elders and the four living creatures, and they fell on their faces before the throne and worshiped God, singing,

"Amen! Blessing and glory and wisdom
and thanksgiving and honor
and power and might
be to our God forever and ever! Amen."

(Revelation 7:11–13)

We can learn a lot about angels by simply reading the Bible.

Angels in the Old Testament

The first part of the Bible is what we call the Old Testament. Pope John Paul II once said that the Old Testament presents images of Angels that are different from those in the New Testament. He wrote: "The Old Testament emphasizes especially the special participation of the angels in the celebration of the glory which the creator receives as a tribute of praise on the part of the created world."[1]

One of the most famous stories in the Old Testament speaks about Abraham and three Angels appearing to him. "The LORD appeared to Abraham by the oaks of Mamre, as he sat at the entrance of his tent in the heat of the day. He looked up and saw three men standing near him. When he saw them, he ran from the tent entrance to meet them, and bowed down to the ground. He said, 'My lord, if I find favor with you, do not pass by your servant" (Genesis 18:1–3).

God had previously told Abraham that he would make a covenant with him. God promised an everlasting covenant throughout future generations and told Abraham he would be the ancestor of a multitude of nations. God also told Abraham, who was ninety-nine years old, that his wife Sarah, who was ninety years old, would have a baby boy and that they would name him Isaac. Abraham and Sarah were faithful to God and believed in his promises even though it was difficult to believe that in their old age they could become parents of a newborn baby. Their son was born the following year, and they named him Isaac. It is through Abraham that thousands of years later a Savior came into the world. That Savior is Jesus Christ!

In other stories of the Old Testament, we see that an Angel was called down from heaven to a woman named Hagar. The Angel told her not to be afraid and saved her and her child Ishmael (Genesis 21:17). Angels also prevented Abraham from sacrificing his son Isaac (Genesis 22:7). We see how Angels protect the just, as it says in Psalms: "For he will command his angels concerning you to guard you in all your ways" (Psalm 91:11). And Angels, we are told, are unceasingly praising God (Isaiah 6:1–4). We repeat the very words of those Angels in church at Mass when we say, "Holy, holy, holy."

One night a man named Jacob had a dream about the Angels. This story also appears in the book of Genesis, in the Old Testament. "Jacob left Beer-sheba and went toward Haran. He came to a certain place and stayed there for the night, because the sun had set. Taking one of the stones of the place, he put it under his head and lay down in that place. And he dreamed that there was a ladder set up on the earth, the top of it reaching heaven; and the angels of God were ascending and descending on it" (Genesis 28:10–12). As God stood beside Jacob and spoke to him, he promised him land and told him that his family would be large and would be blessed. When Jacob woke up, he was very excited that God had been with him in his dream and had given him a great promise. God said he would remain with Jacob wherever he went.

Later, we read how God sends an angel to lead Moses:

I am going to send an angel in front of you, to guard you on the way and to bring you to the place that I have prepared. Be attentive to him and listen to his voice; do not rebel against him, for he will not pardon your transgression; for my name is in him.

But if you listen attentively to his voice and do all that I say, then I will be an enemy to your enemies and a foe to your foes.

(Exodus 23:20–22)

Just as God told Moses to listen to his Angel's "voice," so we must also listen to our Guardian Angel, who leads us to do good. If we pray to our Guardian Angel and ask him to guide us to be good, he will. Our Angel wants us to be in heaven one day with God and all of the saints and Angels!

Later in the Old Testament, in the book of Tobit, the Archangel Raphael appears to Tobias and his wife Sarah, who had just been married. The Archangel says, "I am the Angel Raphael, one of the seven angels who stand ready and enter before the glory of the Lord" (Tobit 12:15). Tobias and Sarah were so afraid that they fell on their faces. Raphael told them not to be afraid: "Peace be with you. Bless God forevermore." Raphael told the couple to praise God each day and speak of him often to others.

Toward the conclusion of the Old Testament, the Psalms proclaim praise to God. In Psalms, we learn about God telling his Angels to help us and to protect us. "The angel of the LORD encamps around those who fear him, and delivers them" (Psalm 34:7). And also, "For he will command his angels concerning you to guard you in all your ways. On their hands they will bear you up, so that you will not dash your foot against a stone" (Psalm 91:11–12).

Angels set a wonderful example for us. They take part as "mighty ones who do his bidding" (who are obedient to God) according to God's plan. "Bless the LORD, O you his angels, you mighty ones who do his bidding, obedient to his spoken word. Bless the LORD, all his hosts, his ministers that do his will" (Psalm 103:20–21).

Then there's the story about Daniel in the lion's den— one of my favorites in all of Holy Scripture.

Then, at break of day, the king got up and hurried to the den of lions. When he came near the den where Daniel was, he cried out anxiously to Daniel, "O Daniel, servant of the living God, has your God whom you faithfully serve been able to deliver you from the lions?" Daniel then said to the king, "O king, live forever! My God sent his angel and shut the lions' mouths so they would not hurt me, because I was found blameless before him; and also before you, O king I have done no wrong" (Daniel 6:19–22).

I love this story because in it God comes through with his Angels to save Daniel. You see, Daniel was accused of breaking a law just because he was praying. Some conspirators told the king that Daniel had been praying, which was against the law. Even though the king didn't like the law, he was stuck with it, and Daniel was thrown to the lions for punishment. After the Angel saved Daniel from the lions, he was freed from the lions' den, and the people who accused Daniel were punished by the king.

Angels in the New Testament

There is a difference between the Old and New Testaments. The Old Testament is the first part of the Bible. In it we learn about the Jews, or Israelites, and God's promises to them. The stories in the Old Testament lead up to the stories in the New Testament, the second part of the Bible, which tells about Jesus, who brought us a new covenant, or promise, which he gives to all people of every race, not only the Jews.

The Angels in the New Testament are active in Jesus's messianic mission, accompanying him on earth. They bring important messages to chosen people and reassure them of God's plan for them and tell them to not be afraid. We witness all of this, first, and most importantly, in the Gospels as they describe what happened leading up to the birth of Christ.

One day, the Angel Gabriel appeared to an aged priest named Zechariah as he was offering incense to God in the temple, and told him that his elderly wife Elizabeth would have a baby (Luke 1:5–19). Zachariah was very frightened at first. But the Angel reassured him, "Do not be afraid, Zechariah, for your prayer has been heard. Your wife Elizabeth will bear you a son, and you will name him John. You will have joy and gladness, and many will rejoice at his birth, for he will be great in the sight of the Lord" (Luke 1:13–14). Gabriel also told Zechariah that his son John would be filled with the Holy Spirit and that numerous people would turn to God because of him. His son John grew up to be John the Baptist.

Soon after this, the Angel Gabriel appeared to a Jewish teenager named Mary. "In the sixth month the angel Gabriel was sent by God to a town in Galilee called Nazareth, to a virgin engaged to a man whose name was Joseph, of the house of David. The virgin's name was Mary. And he came to her and said, 'Greetings, favored one! The Lord is with you'" (Luke 1:26–28). Mary was astounded at the message but had always been prayerful and faithful and wanted what God wanted, so she responded to the Angel Gabriel, "Here am I, the servant of the Lord; let it be with me according to your word." Then the Angel left her.

God used an Angel to help Saint Joseph too. Saint Joseph was troubled and confused. He was not sure what he should do. An Angel reassured Saint Joseph and told him about God's plan. The Bible says:

Now the birth of Jesus the Messiah took place in this way. When his mother Mary had been engaged to Joseph, but before they lived together, she was found to be with child from the Holy Spirit. Her husband Joseph, being a righteous man and unwilling to expose her to public disgrace, planned to dismiss her quietly. But just when he had resolved to do this, an angel of the Lord appeared to him in a dream and said, "Joseph, son of David, do not be

afraid to take Mary as your wife, for the child conceived in her is from the Holy Spirit. She will bear a son, and you are to name him Jesus, for he will save his people from their sins."
(Matthew 1:18–21)

Later on, at the time of Jesus's birth, an Angel appeared to simple shepherds out in the field tending their sheep. And suddenly a multitude of Angels appeared too and began singing songs of praise to God. The Bible says:

In that region there were shepherds living in the fields, keeping watch over their flock by night. Then an angel of the Lord stood before them, and the glory of the Lord shone around them, and they were terrified. But the angel said to them, "Do not be afraid; for see—I am bringing you good news of great joy for all the people: to you is born this day in the city of David a Savior, who is the Messiah, the Lord. This will be a sign for you: you will find a child wrapped in bands of cloth and lying in a manger." And suddenly there was with the angel a multitude of the heavenly host, praising God and saying,

"Glory to God in the highest heaven,
and on earth peace among those whom he favors!"
(Luke 2:8–14)

Can you imagine what this was like for the shepherds to see and hear the Angels and be told the exciting news about Jesus? How do you think you would feel if this happened to you?

An Angel helped protect the holy family, baby Jesus and his mother Mary and foster father Saint Joseph, from danger. The Angel told them what to do to escape and foil King Herod's evil plan. After the wise men who visited baby Jesus left to go home, an Angel came on the scene. He gave complete instructions to Saint Joseph. The Bible says: "Now after they [the wise men] had left, an angel of the Lord appeared to Joseph in a dream and said, 'Get up, take the child and his mother, and flee to Egypt, and remain there until I tell you; for Herod is about to search for the child, to destroy him'" (Matthew 2:13).

So Saint Joseph woke Mary, and they bundled up baby Jesus very quickly and set out immediately for Egypt. They were safe there and stayed in Egypt until Herod died.

Many years later, Jesus was grown and involved in his public ministry of serving others, teaching, preaching, telling everyone about his Father in heaven and healing people. On one occasion, as Jesus fasted for forty days and nights in the desert,

Angels came to confirm his resistance to the devil (see Matthew 4:11). Later on, when Jesus prayed in Gethsemane, Angels again came to his aid. Jesus was praying to his Father in heaven about what was going to happen when he was put to death. "Then an angel from heaven appeared to him and gave him strength" (Luke 22:43). God took care of his Son, Jesus, through the Angels.

After Jesus died for us on the cross, was buried in the tomb, and was resurrected from the dead, Angels appeared to Mary Magdalene. Just before that happened, an angel in the form of a young man told the women who had gathered at the tomb, "Do not be alarmed; you are looking for Jesus of Nazareth, who was crucified. He has been raised, he is not here. . . . Go, tell his disciples" (Mark 16:6–7). The Bible says:

> *But Mary stood weeping outside the tomb. As she wept, she bent over to look into the tomb; and she saw two angels in white, sitting where the body of Jesus had been lying, one at the head and the other at the feet. They said to her, "Woman, why are you weeping?" She said to them, "They have taken away my Lord, and I do not know where they have laid him." When she had said this, she turned around and saw*

Jesus standing there, but she did not know that it was Jesus. Jesus said to her, "Woman, why are you weeping?"
(John 20:11–15)

After a while, Mary Magdalene realized that she was speaking with Jesus, who had been resurrected from the dead. He asked Mary to tell the disciples that he was going to ascend to his Father in heaven. Mary obeyed and went off to tell the disciples that she had seen Jesus and what he'd be doing. Can you even imagine the joy Mary Magdalene must have felt when she saw Jesus and spoke with him?

When Jesus ascended into heaven, two Angels in white robes appeared to the disciples and comforted them, saying, "This Jesus, who has been taken up from you into heaven, will come in the same way as you saw him go into heaven" (Acts 1:11). The Bible tells us that Jesus "has gone into heaven and is at the right hand of God, with angels, authorities, and powers subject to him" (1 Peter 3:22).

Saint John Paul II pointed out, "It can be therefore said that the angels, as pure spirits, not only participate in the holiness of God himself, in the manner proper to them, but in the key moments they surround Christ and accompany him in the fulfillment of his salvific mission in regard to mankind."[2]

An Angel even rescued Saint Peter from jail! The Bible tells us:

> *The very night before Herod was going to bring him out, Peter bound with two chains, was sleeping between two soldiers, while guards in front of the door were keeping watch over the prison. Suddenly an angel of the Lord appeared and a light shone in the cell. He tapped Peter on the side and woke him, saying, "Get up quickly." And the chains fell off his wrists. The angel said to him, "Fasten your belt and put on your sandals." He did so. Then he said to him, "Wrap your cloak around you and follow me." Peter went out and followed him; he did not realize that what was happening with the angel's help was real; he thought he was seeing a vision. After they had passed the first and second guard, they came before the iron gate leading into the city. It opened for them of its own accord, and they went outside and walked along a lane, when suddenly the angel left him.*
> (Acts 12:6–10)

Saint Peter finally realized that what he was experiencing was real and that he was free. He went to a place where many of his friends were gathered and were praying. They were amazed to see him. He told them what had happened, and then he left to tell the others.

Angels were always doing God's work. An Angel also spoke to Saint Philip. Another assailed Herod with a fatal sickness. Saint Paul was protected in his stormy journey at sea by Angels.

Saints Matthew, Mark, and Luke all tell about Angels accompanying Jesus at his Second Coming: "And they will see 'the Son of Man coming on the clouds of heaven' with power and great glory. And he will send out his angels with a loud trumpet call, and they will gather his elect from the four winds, from one end of heaven to the other" (Matthew 24:30–32).

Angels are mentioned even in the last book of the Bible, called Revelation: "When the Lamb opened the seventh seal, there was silence in heaven for about half an hour. And I saw the seven angels who stand before God, and seven trumpets were given them" (Revelation 8:1–2). And also, "And war broke out in heaven; Michael and his angels fought against the dragon. The dragon and his angels fought back, but they were defeated, and there was no longer any place for them in heaven. The great dragon was thrown down, the ancient serpent, who is called the

Devil and Satan, the deceiver of the whole world—he was thrown down to earth, and his angels were thrown down with him" (Revelation 12:7–9).

Angels are very much a part of the entire Bible because they are so much a part of God's work. It's really incredible to think about the Angels working for God in all their power and glory, obeying God and praising him!

Isn't it amazing that one day you will see countless Angels in heaven?

CHAPTER THREE

WHAT ANGELS LOOK LIKE

"Seraphs were in attendance above him; each had six wings: with two they covered their faces, and with two they covered their feet, and with two they flew."

ISAIAH 6:2

Have you ever wondered what Angels really look like? In truth, they have no body—they are pure, invisible spirits. Yet, when they are sent to earth to help with particular circumstances, they might appear in some visible form for the benefit of those whom they are assisting. For instance, sometimes they appear in human form.

Artists have painted, drawn, and sculpted Angels in a variety of styles. Angels are many times portrayed as children. This is most likely to convey innocence.

Beginning in about the fourth century, Angels were usually illustrated with wings. That's how we usually see them in books, paintings, on the walls of churches, in icons, or in the art of stained-glass windows. The wings might even be the artist's interpretation of their swiftness. An Angel is able to quickly come to our aid. However, this also has roots in Holy Scripture, since some of the people in both the Old and New Testaments of the Bible describe the angels who appeared to them as having wings.

For instance, we know that Isaiah saw a winged Angel. Ezekiel, too, saw visions of winged Angels. Most times when Angels appear, they look like normal people, always men. Sometimes Angels appear all aglow in awesome splendor. Warrior Angels—like the Archangels—are tremendously tall and powerful.

At times, God has used his Angels to appear to people in order to accomplish an important task. Saint Catherine Labouré described her Guardian Angel who woke her up one night in 1830 and asked her to come to the chapel to see the Blessed Mother. Saint Catherine said at first she thought the visitor was a small child, and it was later, after the visit with the Blessed Mother, that she realized without a doubt that the little holy child of dazzling radiance was her Guardian Angel.

In 1916, in Fátima, Portugal, Lúcia Santos and her cousins Francisco and Jacinta Marto were visited by an Angel and later on were privileged to see the Blessed Mother in apparitions. Years later, Lúcia would write about the encounters and messages in her memoirs at the insistence of the bishop. Here she describes the first appearance of the Angel:

And then we began to see, in the distance, above the trees that stretched to the east, a light whiter than snow in the form of a young man, quite transparent, and as brilliant as crystal in the rays of the sun. As he came near we were able to see his features. We were astonished and absorbed and we said nothing to one another. And then he said: "Do not be afraid. I am the angel of peace. Pray with me."[3]

The Angel taught the three peasant children this prayer: "My God, I believe, I adore, I hope, and I love You. I ask pardon for those who do not believe, do not adore, do not hope, and do not love You." We should remember that the Angel asked the children to pray this prayer along *with* him. We can say this prayer daily ourselves, even many times a day, and invite our Guardian Angel to pray it with us.

No matter what an angel looks like, we should remember this: it is possible to encounter Angels without being aware. In Hebrews 13:2 we are reminded, "Do not neglect to show hospitality to strangers, for by doing that some have entertained angels without knowing it." In other words, they don't always look like children, or have wings. Sometimes they appear simply in the form of another human being. So be aware!

CHAPTER FOUR

FALLEN ANGELS

"Beloved, do not believe every spirit,
but test the spirits to see
whether they are from God;
for many false prophets have gone out
into the world."

1 JOHN 4:1

As much as we might not want to think about it, we also need to know about the bad Angels. But there is no need for us to worry because God gives us all of the graces we need in our lives to resist the bad influences and temptations from the bad Angels as well as the assistance of the good Angels to light our way toward heaven.

God has given everyone, including the Angels, the right to choose freely. When God created the Angels, some of them chose freely to reject God, his teachings, and his kingdom, even though they were created by God to be good. Sadly, they chose to become evil.

It might seem hard to understand why spiritual beings created to be very intelligent would choose to turn their backs on God, and because they did were cast into hell. We would think they would be smart enough to know what is best for them. True, they were very smart, but they chose to think too highly of themselves and chose not to care about what it was that God wanted for them. They basically said, "I will not serve!" Their arrogance and pride caused their downfall. We can certainly learn from the bad Angels. Let's not be like them!

Saint John Paul II said, "Instead of accepting a God full of love they rejected him, inspired by a false sense of, self-sufficiency, of aversion and even hatred which is changed into rebellion."[4]

The Angels' rejection of God was irreversible because God created them to be super-intelligent and to be able to see the broadest picture of everything throughout history. They clearly knew the consequences of their bad actions, so they had absolutely no legitimate excuses for choosing to reject God. Thankfully, our sins (which are also a rejection of God) are reversible when we admit to them and ask for forgiveness in the sacrament of confession, where we are cleansed of our sins. But it's best not to enter into sin in the first place. Since God has given us the gift of free choice, we need to choose God, not evil.

We read in the Bible, "And the angels who did not keep their own position, but left their proper dwelling, he has kept in eternal chains in deepest darkness for the judgment of the great day" (Jude 6). Because those Angels decided to become evil, God cast them into hell, where they remain. They were far too intelligent to make such a bad choice, so they have to suffer in hell eternally. The bad Angels are usually referred to as demons. The head of the bad Angels is Satan, the devil. He has been referred to as a lion, an evil one, a dragon, a serpent, and more.

We should be aware that Satan rejected God from the beginning and chooses to do harm to others, trying to get people away from believing in God. The Bible tells us that he is a "liar and the father of lies" (John 8:44). Sometimes the way Satan is able to influence people to do evil things is by getting them to believe that he and hell do not exist and that they have nothing to fear in doing bad things because there will be no eternal punishment. But we know better than that. Our faithful prayers and the help of the good Angels will keep us from falling for the devil's tricks. Let's be sure to pray every day.

Jesus taught us the prayer called the Our Father. It reminds us that we are exposed to the evil one on our journey through life. Pray the Our Father prayer slowly soon, and think about the words. With the gift of faith that God gives us, we can pray this prayer and be confident that God will help us in the battle on earth of good versus evil.

Our Church teaches us to stay faithful to God's teachings, to remain prayerful in our everyday lives, and to choose to do good—always. We can call on the good Angels at any time for their assistance in resisting temptations to do something that is not good. The good Angels will help us to lead holy lives. We should call on them each day.

CHAPTER FIVE

THE ARCHANGELS

*"I am Gabriel. I stand in the presence of God,
and I have been sent to speak to you and to
bring you this good news."*

LUKE 1:19

hree Archangels are mentioned by name
in the Bible. They are Michael, Gabriel,
and Raphael. All three of the Archangels'
activities reflect the question in the Bible, "Are not all
angels spirits in the divine service, sent to serve for the
sake of those who are to inherit salvation?" (Hebrews
1:14).

There might be other archangels in heaven too, but
we don't know their names. After all, the Archangel

Raphael told Tobias and Sarah, "I am the angel Raphael, one of the seven angels who stand ready and enter before the glory of the Lord" (Tobit 12:15).

Saint Michael the Archangel

Saint Michael is the chief angel. His name means, "Who is like God?" He is known as a great protector against the devil and evil. He is mentioned in the Bible in the book of Jude (verse 9) and in the book of Daniel (10:13). Also as was said in chapter 2, he is mentioned in Revelation (12:7–9), which describes a war in heaven with Michael leading his army of Angels in a battle against Satan (the devil) and his bad Angels. Satan is thrown out of heaven and down to earth. For this reason, because of his power and reputation for holiness, we are encouraged to say a prayer to Saint Michael for protection (prayers to him are in chapter 8).

Saint Gabriel the Archangel

Saint Gabriel is known as perhaps the most important messenger of God in history. He is mentioned in the Old Testament in the book of Daniel (8:16 and 9:21), where he is described as God's messenger to Daniel, as well as in the New Testament in Luke's Gospel (1:19–26). His name means "my power is God" or "power of God."

The Archangel Gabriel announced the future births of John the Baptist and Jesus. In Luke's Gospel, Gabriel appears to Zechariah and tells him that his wife Elizabeth will have a baby (Luke 1:5–19). Zachariah is terrified. But the archangel tells him, "Do not be afraid, Zechariah, for your prayer has been heard. Your wife Elizabeth will bear you a son, and you will name him John. You will have joy and gladness, and many will rejoice at his birth, for he will be great in the sight of the Lord" (Luke 1:13–15). Saint Gabriel also tells him that John will be filled with the Holy Spirit and will turn many people to God. Then Gabriel tells Zechariah John's name.

He says, "I am Gabriel. I stand in the presence of God, and I have been sent to speak to you and tell you the good news" (Luke 1:19). The pregnancy was indeed miraculous. Elizabeth had not been able to bear children before this time.

It was also Gabriel who then visited the Jewish teenager Mary, who would later be called the Blessed Mother. Gabriel told her she would have a miraculous pregnancy and would be blessed among women to be the Mother of the "Son of God." He told Mary that her cousin Elizabeth was also expecting a baby. "For nothing will be impossible with God" (Luke 1:37).

Mary accepted the blessing and then traveled to visit her cousin Elizabeth, who needed her help and companionship.

Saint Raphael the Archangel

Saint Raphael is the third archangel. His name in Hebrew means "God heals." He is mentioned in the book of Tobit in the Bible.

Raphael is sent from heaven to help two Jewish people who are exiled in a place called Nineveh. A blind Israelite named Tobit is given his sight miraculously, and a young woman named Sarah is relieved of her suffering. Both were faithful and prayerful people. Because of their prayerful good life, God sent Saint Raphael to help them. Tobit sent his son, Tobias, to a place called Media. Raphael joined him on this journey, but Tobias didn't know Raphael was an Angel because Raphael was disguised as a man named Azariah. All along the journey, Saint Raphael protected Tobias and guided him with much wisdom. His instructions to Tobias eventually delivered Sarah, who was in Media, from an evil demon.

Tobias and the young woman Sarah got married and were very happy and praised God. The instructions that the Angel gave Tobias also healed his father, Tobit, of his blindness when Tobias returned home. Then the Archangel Raphael revealed who he was: "I am Raphael, one of the seven angels who stand ready and enter before the glory of the Lord" (Tobit 12:15). He told them that he was sent to them to test their faith and to heal them. He explained that he had brought their prayers to God. Saint Raphael told them to not be afraid and to "Bless God forevermore. . . . Bless him each and every day; sing his praises" (Tobit 12:18). Then he returned to heaven because his work was complete.

Saint Gregory the Great once said that Saint Raphael is the "great medicine of God." He is known as the healing Angel. We can pray to Saint Raphael for good health and strength for our bodies and our souls.

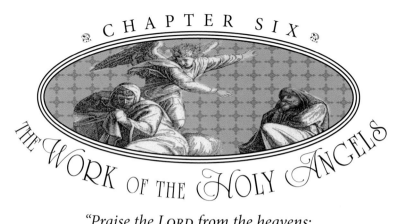

CHAPTER SIX

THE WORK OF THE HOLY ANGELS

"Praise the LORD from the heavens;
praise him in the heights!
Praise him all his angels."

PSALM 148:1-2

The Greek word for angel, *angelos*, means "one sent." The Old Testament uses the Hebrew term *malak Elohim* or *malak YHWH*, which means "messenger of God" or "messenger of the Lord." Angels have always been given a special ministry of spreading God's messages to human beings.

Angels have a lot of important jobs. They are also adorers of God, guardians of God, ambassadors of God, guides, and mediators.

But the principal job of the Angels in heaven is to adore God and praise him. They will do this for eternity. Someday we will be there beside them, doing it too.

Even as the Angels in heaven are adoring God, they are praying and helping us spiritually with our journey toward heaven. Angels are also assigned the job of protecting people and caring for their salvation. Saint Thomas Aquinas believed that they help us most of all toward this by enlightening our minds with holy ideas. We are very blessed that they do.

Our Church teaches us,

> From its beginning to death human life is surrounded by their [the Angels'] watchful care and intercession. "Beside each believer stands an angel as protector and shepherd leading him to life." Already here on earth the Christian life shares by faith in the blessed company of angels and men united in God. (Catechism of the Catholic Church, §336)

Saint John Paul II has said the Angels "are called from the beginning, by virtue of their intelligence, to know the truth and to love the good which they know in truth in a more full and perfect way than is possible to man."[5] The Angels are far more intelligent than anyone we know.

It is very fascinating to know that the Angels always see the face of God—always! Jesus told us this. He explained that they "continually see the face of my Father in heaven" (Matthew 18:10). This means that the Angels are always in adoration of God. Even as they are doing a task on earth, they can still see God. It's a mystery and a miracle.

At each and every Catholic Mass (each day and each hour all around the world) the priest invites the Angels and Archangels to sing the glory of God. Do you know that when you are at Mass Angels are there too? They are around the altar. It's incredible to think about this. But, truly, Angels are everywhere!

At every Sunday Mass we recite the Nicene Creed (dating from the year 325), and we reaffirm our belief in the creation and existence of Angels when we say, "We believe in one God, the Father Almighty, maker of heaven and earth, of all that is seen and unseen (or, in other translations, "of all things visible and invisible").

We are reminded of our belief in the existence of the Angels in another prayer called the *Credo of the People of God* (Pope Paul VI, June 20, 1968): "We believe in one God, the Father, the Son and the Holy Spirit, Creator of what is visible—such as this world where we live out our lives—and of the invisible—such as the pure spirits which are also called angels."

The Bible also tells us that the Angels' tasks are aimed at protecting and helping not only people like us but entire nations (Daniel 10:13–21).

Most of all, the Church teaches us that Angels are our guardians in life. And we should show honor to our Guardian Angels. "These pure Spirits most nearly resemble God and yet are not dissimilar to man, having intelligence and will like us. They are God's intermediaries between the God they see and mankind whom they are entrusted to lead to the same Beatific Vision," we are told by theologian and Servant of God Father John A. Hardon, sj.[6]

Saint Ambrose reminds us to ask for protection from the Angels and not to just take them for granted. He specifically says, "The servants of Christ are protected by invisible, rather than visible beings. But if these guard you, they do so because they have been summoned by your prayer." So let's remember to ask for the Angels' help.[7]

CHAPTER SEVEN

ANGELS, OUR FRIENDS

"He will command his angels concerning you
to guard you in all your ways.
On their hands they will bear you up,
so that you will not dash your foot
against a stone."

PSALM 91:11–13

ouldn't you like to keep company with the incredible angelic friends who unceasingly glorify God and who have always been an important part of salvation history? They protected Jesus throughout his life, announcing heaven's plans and guiding and protecting the faithful. They can help you too!

It was Saint Francis de Sales who said, "Make friends with the angels, who though invisible are always with you. . . . Often invoke them, constantly praise them, and make good use of their help and assistance in all your temporal and spiritual affairs."[8]

Get in the habit of speaking with your Guardian Angel often. When you wake up in the morning, pray to your Guardian Angel first thing. Ask him to take care of you and your family and to guide you to be good all day. Throughout the day, you can also keep company with your Guardian Angel by speaking with him in prayer, asking him to help you with whatever you are doing and to guide you closer to God. Before you go to sleep at night, talk to your Angel again. Ask for his protection during the night.

Many of the saints have listened closely to their Guardian Angels. Saint Padre Pio remarked, "What a consolation it is to know one is always in the care of a celestial spirit, who does not abandon us (how admirable) even when we disgust God! How sweet is this great truth for the believer!"[9] Saint Josemaria Escriva teaches us, "Have confidence in your guardian angel. Treat him as a lifelong friend—that is what he is—and he will render you a thousand services in ordinary affairs each day."[10]

Each Guardian Angel takes on three additional, spiritual roles as well. They help us on our way toward

peace,

penitence, and

prayer.

Our Guardian Angel brings us peace when we are troubled, just as the Angels came to the assistance of Jesus when he prayed in the Garden of Gethsemane. Ask your Angel for this help now, or whenever you feel that you need it.

As the Angel of penitence, our Guardian Angel also possesses the role of disciplining us when we turn away from God. He takes part in bringing us into the graces of our faith by helping us to confess and restore our soul to health after sinning.

And as our Guardian Angel of prayer, he presents all of our prayers to God. Knowing what our Guardian Angels are busy doing for us should encourage us to continually call on our true friend, confident that he will care for us and guide us closer and closer to heaven.

Theologian and Servant of God Father John A. Hardon, sj, says, "Catholics should pray, soliciting our Angels' continued protection and asking them to present our prayers to God."[11] Imagine that—our

Angels present our prayers to God! Don't hesitate to pray to your Guardian Angel.

Saint John Paul II reminded us to be watchful so we don't fall for the evil temptations of the devil, and he encouraged us to feel confident in our Guardian Angel's protection when we call on him.

And while the existence of the wicked angels requires of us that we be watchful so as not to yield to their empty promises, we are certain that the victorious power of Christ the Redeemer enfolds our lives, so that we ourselves may overcome these spirits. In this, we are powerfully helped by the good angels, messengers of God's love, to whom, taught by the tradition of the Church, we address our prayer: "Angel of God, who are my guardian, enlighten, guard, govern and guide me, who have been entrusted to you by the heavenly goodness. Amen."[12]

Prayers, Commemoration, and Patronages

"Bless the Lord, O you his angels,
you mighty ones who do his bidding,
obedient to his spoken word."

PSALM 103:20

Angel Feast Days

A feast day is a day on which we remember Jesus, Mary, an Angel, or a saint in a special way. One way is by going to Mass or praying certain prayers. Celebrating the feast days helps us to grow in our faith and become more familiar with and close to our friends in heaven.

On September 29 we observe a special feast day for the three Archangels: Michael, Raphael, and Gabriel.

In some parts of the world, September 29 is the feast of Saint Michael, Saint Gabriel's feast day is observed on March 24, and Saint Raphael is observed on October 24. On October 2 we observe a special feast day for the Guardian Angels.

Try to do something special on these feast days to remember the Angels of the Bible, or your own Guardian Angel. You can pray specific prayers and enjoy a special dinner or dessert in their honor. Draw or paint a picture or write a story about one of the Archangels. Tell your friends and family about the importance of Angels. If you can, try to go to Mass on these days.

What do you think is the most interesting trait of an Angel? How do you think the Angels help you personally?

Angel Shrines

Even though we usually can't see Angels, it's very good to honor them with our prayers and also by creating places called shrines. Visiting shrines dedicated to the Angels can help us grow in our faith and draw our attention to the Angels in a deeper way.

Many cities and corporations have adopted Angels as their patrons. There are impressive shrines in the honor of many angel saints in many parts of the world. Some of the most famous ones include the following:

Chapel of the Angels in Beit Sahur, Palestine, (a mile from Bethlehem) designed by Antonio Barlucci and built by Canadian Catholics.

Mont-Saint-Michel in Normandy, France, where Archangel Michael is honored.

San Michele della Chiusa in Piedmont, Italy where Archangel Michael is honored.

San Michele Gargano in Apulia, Italy where Archangel Michael is honored.

Have you ever been to a shrine to the Angels? You can make your own shrine by placing an Angel statue on a table or shelf, or by hanging an image of an Angel on the wall (with your parents' permission). Then make a point of saying a prayer to your Guardian Angel and all of the Angels at your little shrine every day.

Special Prayers to the Angels

ANGEL OF GOD

O angel of God, my guardian dear,
To whom his love commits me here,
Ever this day, be at my side,
To watch and guard, to rule and guide.
Amen

This popular ancient prayer carries a partial indulgence. Do you know what that is?

TO ONE'S GUARDIAN ANGEL

Angel of God,
Whom God has appointed to be my protector
Against all things evil:
Be always at my side, and keep me aware of
Your presence as God's messenger to me all
The days of my life, for my good.
Pray for me this day and every day of my life in this
world.
Amen.

TO ALL THE ANGELS

All you holy angels and archangels,
thrones and dominations,
principalities and powers,
the virtues of heaven,
cherubim and seraphim,
praise the Lord forever.
Amen.

FOR ANGEL PRESENCE AT HOME

O Lord, we ask you to visit this home

And drive from it all it all the snares of the enemy.

Let your holy angels dwell here, to preserve us in
peace;

And may your blessings be upon us forever,

Through our Lord Jesus Christ. Amen.[13]

The Angelus

The Angelus is an ancient prayer in honor of the occasion when the Archangel Gabriel visited Mary to tell her she would become the Mother of God. Traditionally, church bells are rung in three bursts of three chimes, pausing slightly between rings. Then nine strokes of bells follow. This is done at 6 AM, noon, and 6 PM every day at many Catholic churches. This tradition of ringing the church bells and praying the Angelus at these times comes from a monastic practice of praying. The bells alerted people in the villages to stop for a moment from their work to pray three Hail Marys in honor of Mary becoming Jesus's mother. Later on, in the year 1612, verses were added to the Hail Marys to form the prayer we now pray today.

❧

The Angel of the Lord declared to Mary:

And she conceived of the Holy Spirit.

Hail Mary, full of grace, the Lord is with thee; blessed art thou among women and blessed is the fruit of thy womb, Jesus. Holy Mary, Mother of God, pray for us sinners, now and at the hour of our death. Amen.

Behold the handmaid of the Lord: Be it done unto me according to Thy word.

Hail Mary . . .

And the Word was made Flesh: And dwelt among us.

Hail Mary . . .

Pray for us, O Holy Mother of God, that we may be made worthy of the promises of Christ.

Let us pray:

Pour forth, we beseech Thee, O Lord, Thy grace into our hearts; that we, to whom the incarnation of Christ, Thy Son, was made known by the message of an Angel, may by His Passion and Cross be brought to the glory of His Resurrection, through the same Christ Our Lord.

Amen.

Praying the Angelus reminds us of the Annunciation, that miraculous event when the Angel Gabriel appeared to Mary with magnificent news (Luke 1:26–38). He told Mary, a humble and faithful young woman, that God desired that she be the mother of his Son, our Lord Jesus Christ.

Prayers of the Angel at Fátima

The Angel appeared three times to the children at Fátima. During the first encounter the Angel said, Do not be afraid. I am the angel of peace. Pray with me."

Then the Angel taught the three children to pray this prayer, telling them to pray it three times:

My God, I believe, I adore, I hope, and I love You. I ask pardon for those who do not believe, do not adore, do not hope, and do not love You.

During the third apparition to the children in 1916, with the Blessed Sacrament suspended in the air, the Angel of Peace stretched out with his face on the ground and recited this prayer.

Oh Most Holy Trinity,

Father, Son, and Holy Spirit,

I adore Thee profoundly.

I offer Thee the most precious Body, Blood, Soul
and Divinity

of Jesus Christ, present in all the tabernacles of
the world,

in reparation for the outrages, sacrileges and

indifferences by which He is offended.

By the infinite merits of the Sacred Heart of Jesus

and the Immaculate Heart of Mary,

I beg the conversion of poor sinners.

Amen.

ANGEL SENT BY GOD TO GUIDE ME

Angel sent by God to guide me,

Be my light and walk beside me;

Be my guardian and protect me; on the paths of
life direct me.[14]

SLEEP MY CHILD,
LET PEACE ATTEND THEE

Sleep my child, let peace attend thee,

All through the night,

Guardian Angels God will send thee,

All through the night.

[from a Welsh lullaby]

NOW THE DAY IS OVER

Child of hope and promise,
May you walk in the light.
May the Angels guard you
Through the dark of the night.
[an American classic lullaby]

SAINT MICHAEL THE ARCHANGEL

St. Michael, the Archangel, defend us in battle; be our defense against the wickedness and snares of the devil. May God rebuke him, we humbly pray; and do thou, O Prince of the heavenly host, by the power of God, thrust into hell Satan and the other evil spirits who prowl about the world seeking the ruin of souls. Amen.

On October 13, 1884, after saying Mass for a group of cardinals, Pope Leo XIII felt deeply inspired to write a prayer to Saint Michael asking for his protection for the Church. Pope Leo XIII had just mystically witnessed a confrontation between Jesus and Satan. The prayer was long and descriptive.

In 1886, Pope Leo XIII made a decree that the prayer be said after all low Masses. Later, in 1934, a shorter version of the prayer was written (which we see above) and it was prayed after every low Mass said throughout the world. In 1970, the practice of praying the prayer directly after Mass was discontinued. But Saint John Paul II said, "I invite you all not to forget it. Pray it so as to be helped in the battle against forces of darkness and against the spirit of the world."

❧

ANOTHER PRAYER TO SAINT MICHAEL

Most glorious prince of the heavenly armies, Saint
Michael the archangel,

defend us in battle against principalities and powers,

against rulers of this world of darkness,

against the spirits of wickedness in the high places
(Ephesians 6:12).

come to the assistance of men whom God has
created to his likeness

And whom he has redeemed at a great price from
the tyranny of the devil.

Holy Church venerates you as her guardian and
protector;

to you the Lord has entrusted the souls of the
redeemed to be led into heaven.

Pray therefore the God of peace to crush Satan
beneath our feet,

that he no longer retain men captive and do injury
to the Church.

Offer our prayers to the Most High,

that without delay they may draw his mercy down
upon us;

take hold of "the dragon, the old serpent, which is
the devil and Satan,"

bind him and cast him into the bottomless pit

"so that he may no longer seduce the nations" (Revelation 20:2).

❧

SAINT RAPHAEL THE ARCHANGEL

O God,

send the Archangel Raphael to our assistance.

May he who stands forever praising you

at your throne

present our humble petitions to be blessed by you.

Through Christ our Lord.

Amen.

❧

SAINT GABRIEL THE ARCHANGEL

O God,
who from among all your angels
chose the Archangel Gabriel
to announce the mystery of the Incarnation,
mercifully grant that we
who solemnly remember him on earth
may feel the benefits of his
patronage in heaven,
who lives and reigns for ever and ever.
Amen.

❦

HEALING PRAYER TO SAINT RAPHAEL

Glorious archangel Saint Raphael, great prince of the heavenly court, you are illustrious for your gifts of wisdom and grace. You are a guide to those who journey by land or sea or air, consoler of the afflicted, and refuge of sinners.

I beg you, assist me in all my needs and in all the sufferings of this life, as once you helped the young Tobias on his travels. Because you are the "medicine of God" I humbly pray you to heal the many infirmities of my soul and the ills that afflict my body. I especially ask of you the favor of (here mention your special intention) and the great grace of purity to prepare me to be the temple of the Holy Spirit. Amen.

❧

PRAYER TO SAINT GABRIEL FOR STRENGTH

Blessed Saint Gabriel, archangel,

We beseech you to intercede for us at the throne of divine mercy;

As you announced the mystery of the Incarnation to Mary,

So through your prayers may we receive strength of faith and courage of spirit,

And thus find favor with God and redemption through Christ our Lord.

May we sing the praise of God our Savior with the angels and saints

In heaven for ever and ever. Amen.[15]

❧

PRAYER TO SAINT RAPHAEL
FOR HAPPY MEETINGS

O Raphael, lead us towards those we are waiting for, those who are waiting for us: Raphael, angel of happy meeting, lead us by the hand toward those we are looking for. May all our movements be guided by your light and transfigured with your joy.

Angel, guide of Tobias, lay the request we now address to you at the feet of him on whose unveiled face you are privileged to gaze.

Lonely and tired, crushed by the separations and sorrows of life, we feel the need of calling you and of pleading for the protection of your wings,

so we may not be as strangers in the province of
    joy,
all ignorant of the concerns of our country.
Remember the weak, you who are strong,
you whose home lies behind the region of thunder,
in a land that is always peaceful,
always serene and bright with resplendent glory
    of God.

[attributed to Ernest Hello, 1964]

SAINT GERTRUDE'S
GUARDIAN ANGEL PRAYER

O most holy angel of God, appointed by God to be my guardian, I give you thanks for all the benefits which you have ever bestowed on me in body and in soul. I praise and glorify you that you condescended to assist me with such patient fidelity, and to defend me against all the assaults of my enemies. Blessed be the hour in which you were assigned me for my guardian, my defender, and my patron. In acknowledgment and return for all your loving ministries to me, I offer you the infinitely precious and noble heart of Jesus, and firmly purpose to obey you henceforward, and most faithfully to serve my God. Amen.

❧

CONCLUSION

Now that you've read *Angels for Kids* and learned all about Angels, you can be more aware of their holy work all around you. You'll know that each time you go to Mass, holy Angels are all around the altar giving praise and glory to God. You can remember that you have a faithful Angel friend assigned to you by God to be your attentive companion all throughout your life. Even if you forget about your Angel, he won't forget about you. But it's best to try to remember him each day and ask him for his help and protection. He is more like a family member than merely a friend.

Saint Padre Pio was known to speak to his Guardian Angel often. He once told someone, "Develop the beautiful habit of always thinking of him; that near us is a celestial spirit, who, from the cradle to the tomb, does not leave us for an instant, guides us, protects us as a friend, a brother; will always be a consolation to us especially in our saddest moments. . . . This good Angel prays for you; offers to God all the good works you accomplish; your holy and pure desires. . . . Do not forget this invisible companion, always present to listen to you; always ready to console you."[16]

Take some time, perhaps with your family, to look up the areas of the Bible that are noted throughout this book to experience reading about and learning from the Angels and their stories in the Bible.

God loves us so much that he gave us the gift of Angels. Let's show God that we are thankful for his wonderful gift by praying to our Guardian Angels every day and listening carefully to the good inspirations they give us to stay away from sin and to always do good to please God.

One day you will receive the most amazing blessing in meeting your Guardian Angel and all of the remarkable Angels in heaven! And for now, you can feel confident knowing that even though you can't see the Angels, they are indeed present and they deeply care about you and me.

I'm praying that you will continue to grow in your faith each and every day and that through your prayers and God's loving grace you will come closer to God and be a wonderful Christian example to others. God bless you!

❈ ACKNOWLEDGMENTS ❈

With a grateful heart to all who have guided me, prayed for me, and loved me throughout my life: my family and friends, especially my parents, Eugene Joseph and Alexandra Mary Cooper; my brothers and sisters, Alice Jean, Gene, Gary, Barbara, Tim, Michael, and David; and my friend Fr. Bill C. Smith (now in Heaven), who knew of my desire to write a book about the holy Angels—I am eternally indebted. And, of course, I thank my Guardian Angel!

My children have always been my utmost vocation. I love you, Justin, Chaldea, Jessica, Joseph, and Mary-Catherine! My husband, David, the wind beneath my wings, thank you for your love and support!

Heartfelt thanks to Jon M. Sweeney and the wonderful team at Paraclete Press for their partnership in getting this book out to you! Loving prayers for all who are connected through my books, talks, and pilgrimages—thank you for joining me in prayer on the spectacular journey that leads to eternal life!